WE CAN DRAW

WE CAN DRAW DINOSAURS

Corina Jeffries

WINDMILL BOOKS™
New York

Published in 2023 by Windmill Books, an Imprint of Rosen Publishing
29 East 21st Street, New York, NY 10010

Portions of this work were originally authored by Laura Murawski and published as *How to Draw Dinosaurs*. All new material in this edition authored by Corina Jeffries.

Library of Congress Cataloging-in-Publication Data
Names: Jeffries, Corina, author.
Title: We can draw dinosaurs / Corina Jeffries.
Description: New York : Windmill Books, [2023] | Series: We can draw | Includes index. | Audience: Grades 2-3
Identifiers: LCCN 2021058889 (print) | LCCN 2021058890 (ebook) | ISBN 9781508198109 (library binding) | ISBN 9781508198086 (paperback) | ISBN 9781508198093 (set) | ISBN 9781508198116 (ebook)
Subjects: LCSH: Dinosaurs in art–Juvenile literature. | Drawing–Technique–Juvenile literature.
Classification: LCC NC780.5 .J44 2023 (print) | LCC NC780.5 (ebook) | DDC 743.6–dc23/eng/20220104
LC record available at https://lccn.loc.gov/2021058889
LC ebook record available at https://lccn.loc.gov/2021058890

Designer: Leslie Taylor
Editor: Caitie McAneney

Photo credits: Cover and p. 1 (dinosaur), pp. 10, 16, 18, 20 Daniel Eskridge/Shutterstock.com; series artwork (pencils) suriya yapin/Shutterstock.com; series artwork (art table) insta_photos/Shutterstock.com; series artwork (banner) Kathy Kiselova/Shutterstock.com; series artwork (scribbles) mart/Shutterstock.com; p. 4 Herschel Hoffmeyer/Shutterstock.com; p. 5 (pencils) ILLUSTOR STUDIO/Shutterstock.com; p. 5 (child) George Rudy/Shutterstock.com; p. 6 freestyle images/Shuttertstock.com; p. 8 kamomeen/Shutterstock.com; p. 12 Michael Rosskothen/Shutterstock.com; p. 14 Dotted Yeti/Shutterstock.com.

Manufactured in the United States of America

CPSIA compliance information: Batch #CSWM23: For further information contact Rosen Publishing, New York, New York at 1-800-237-9932.

CONTENTS

DISCOVER AND DRAW DINOSAURS

Did you know that the word "dinosaur" comes from the Greek words that mean "terrible lizard"? These amazing creatures may have lived millions of years ago, but there's still plenty to discover about them. Paleontologists are scientists who study **fossils**. They study the things dinosaurs left behind to discover more about them.

Dinosaurs existed during the **Mesozoic era**, which is divided into three periods: the Triassic (251–201 million years ago), the Jurassic (201–145 million years ago), and the Cretaceous (145–66 million years ago). This book highlights many different dinosaurs—from **fierce** hunters to peaceful plant-eaters. You can learn more about each dinosaur before you start drawing.

Discovering facts about dinosaurs can make drawing them more fun! First, you'll learn about the fearsome *Tyrannosaurus rex*. Follow each step in the instructions carefully to create your very own prehistoric predator!

Gather your drawing materials!

You'll need a pencil, pencil sharpener, eraser, and paper. You might want to make your drawings in a sketch pad.

DISCOVER TYRANNOSUARUS REX

One of the most fearsome dinosaurs was *Tyrannosaurus rex*, also called *T. rex*. This powerful dinosaur was a carnivore, or meat-eater. In fact, its name means "**tyrant** lizard king" in Greek. *T. rex* lived about 80 million years ago during the Late Cretaceous period.

Standing upright, an adult *T. rex* was about 21 feet (6.4 m) tall. *T. rex* walked on two strong hind, or back, legs. Each foot had three toes with pointed claws and a very sharp fourth claw that pointed backward. Its arms were relatively small, but very strong. *T. rex* had powerful jaws with 60 massive teeth to take big bites out of its **prey**. The most complete *T. rex* skeleton, named SUE, was found in 1990 in South Dakota.

Tyrannosaurus rex was one of the last dinosaurs to **evolve** before dinosaurs became extinct, or died out.

1

To start, draw a large oval to begin the body of *Tyrannosaurus rex*.

2

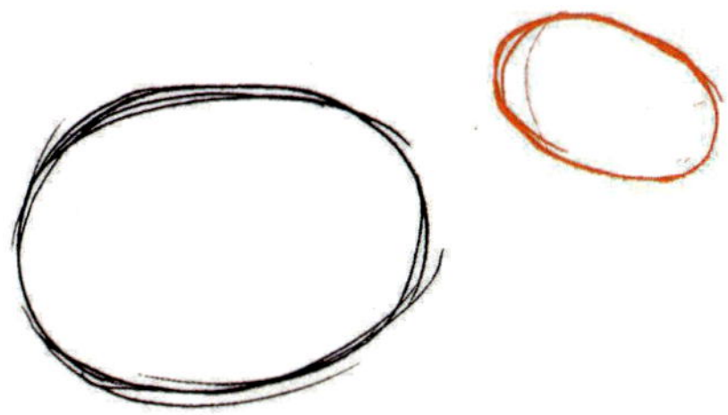

To the upper right of the large oval, draw a small, tilted oval for the head.

3

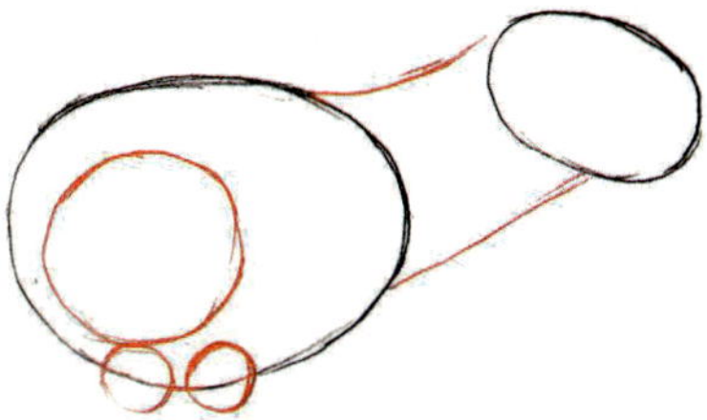

To make the neck, join the ovals with two curved lines. Add a circle inside and of the large oval as shown here. To begin the legs, draw two small circles under the large circle.

4

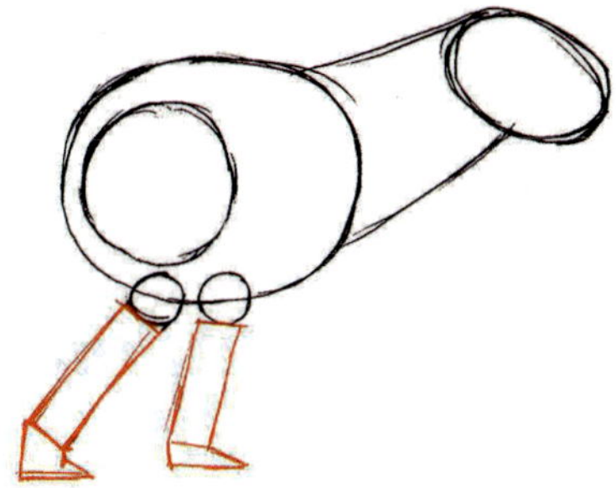

Next, draw two rectangles coming from the small circles. Make two angular shapes beneath the rectangles for the feet.

5

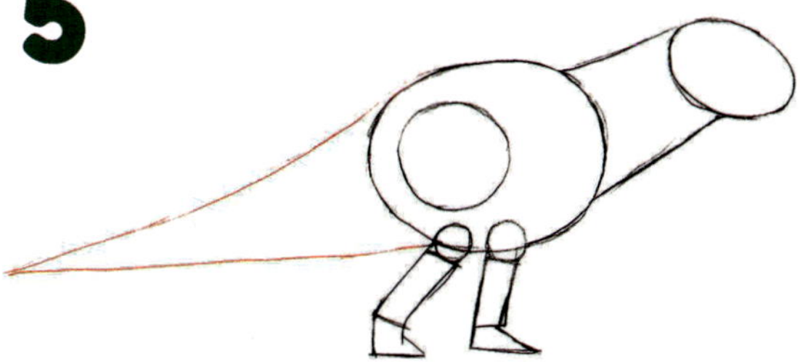

To make the tail, draw two long lines out from the back of the body that meet together at a point.

6

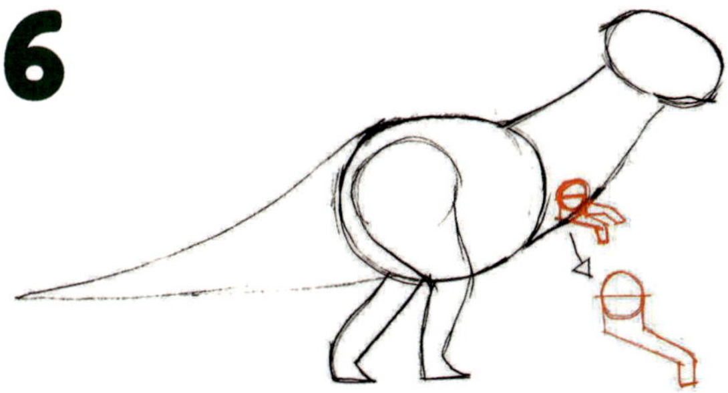

To clean up the lines of the legs, join the shapes with curved lines, and erase any extra lines. To draw the dinosaur's tiny arms, first draw a circle, and then draw the shape below the circle as shown.

7

Finish the face by drawing an open mouth, teeth, an eye, and a nostril. Add details to the feet and arms as shown. Erase any extra lines. That's one terrific *T. rex*!

DISCOVER VELOCIRAPTOR

One of the fastest dinosaurs ever to live was *Velociraptor*. In fact, its name means "swift robber" in Latin. This **raptor** could run up to 24 miles (39 km) per hour. It had clawed hands that were perfect for grabbing things, such as eggs, from the nests of larger dinosaurs! Scientists also believe *Velociraptor* was one of the smartest dinosaurs. The dinosaur's body was small, but its brain was relatively large.

Velociraptor lived in the Late Cretaceous period. Its small body helped it move fast. It was only about 6 feet (1.8 m) long and about 3 feet (0.9 m) tall. *Velociraptor* was a carnivore, probably hunting small lizards, baby dinosaurs, and small **mammals**. It had sharp teeth and a claw on each foot for hunting.

Velociraptor is thought to have had feathers like a bird but could not fly.

1

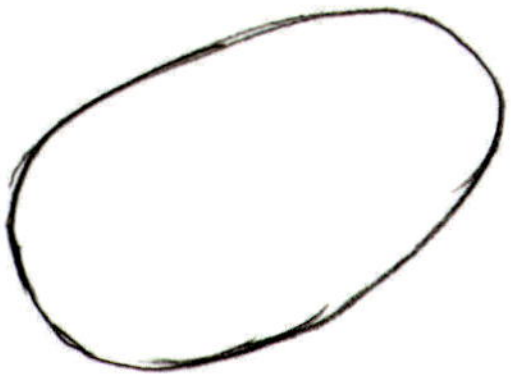

To begin, make a large oval for the body of *Velociraptor*.

2

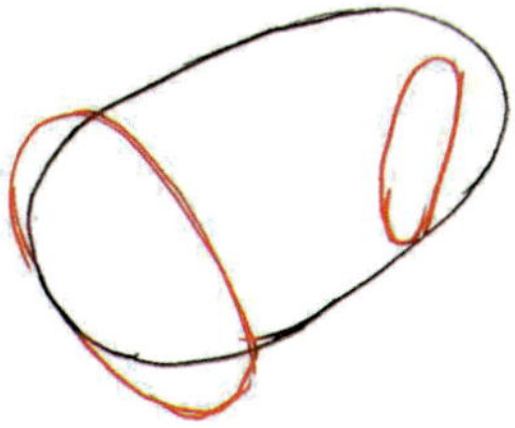

For the legs, draw two smaller, thinner ovals, tilted as shown in this illustration.

3

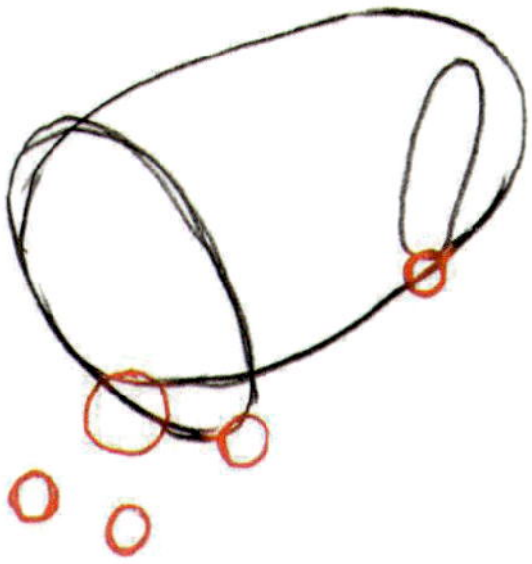

Continue drawing the legs by making five small circles as shown here.

4

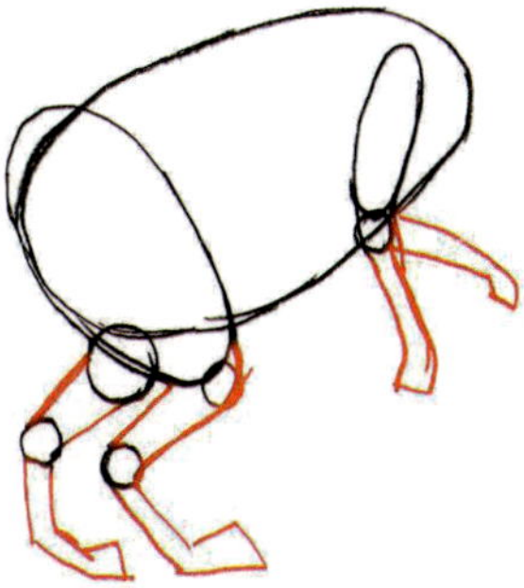

Next, complete the legs by drawing lines to connect the circles. Add angular shapes for the feet and hands.

5

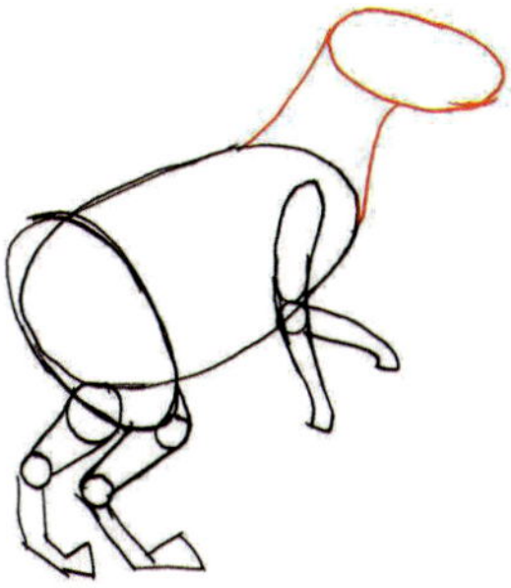

Draw an oval above and to the right of the body for the head. Use two curved lines to join this oval to the body.

6

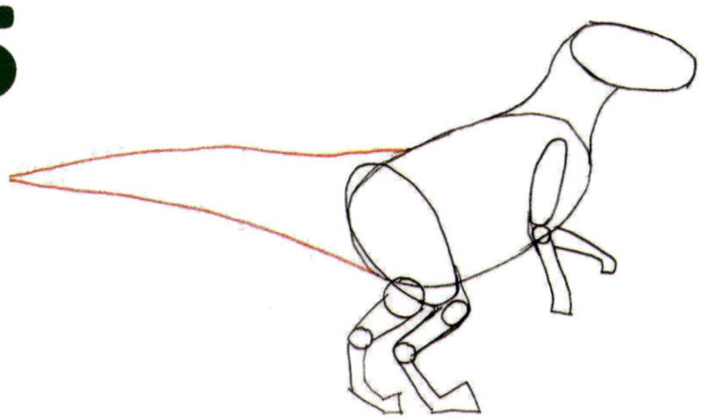

To make the tail, draw two long, curved lines from the back of the body. Notice how these lines come to a point at the end.

7

Curve the line of its back and head. Add the eye, nose, and mouth. Add claws to the hands and feet as shown. The center claws on the back feet should be longer.

8

Add sharp teeth and details to the face. Erase any extra lines. Now, draw thin, upside-down triangles along the back, and shade them in to create a striped effect.

DISCOVER DEINONYCHUS

Another dangerous dinosaur and great hunter was *Deinonychus*. Like *Velociraptor*, *Deinonychus* was a feathered raptor from the Cretaceous period. However, *Velociraptor* lived in today's central and eastern Asia in the Late Cretaceous period, and *Deinonychus* lived in what is today western North America in the Early Cretaceous period. While *Velociraptor* was relatively small, *Deinonychus* measured about 10 feet (3 m) long and 6 feet (1.8 m) tall,

Deinonychus was known for its big, curved claws. In fact, its name means "terrible claw." On the second toe of each back foot was a 5-inch (12.7 cm) claw shaped like a curved knife! It may have used these back claws to tear open the bellies of its prey. Deinonychus was the model for the raptors in the 1993 movie *Jurassic Park*.

The combination of its size, speed, cleverness, and claws made *Deinonychus* very deadly.

1

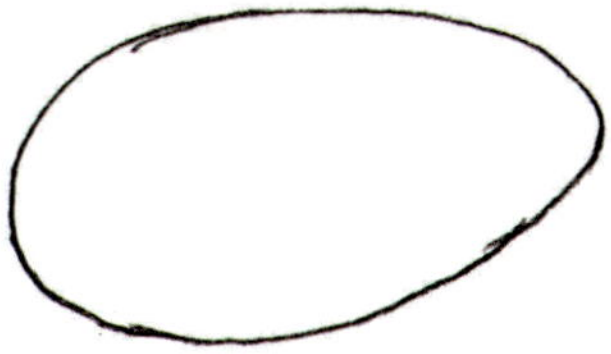

To begin, draw a large oval to make the body of the *Deinonychus*.

2

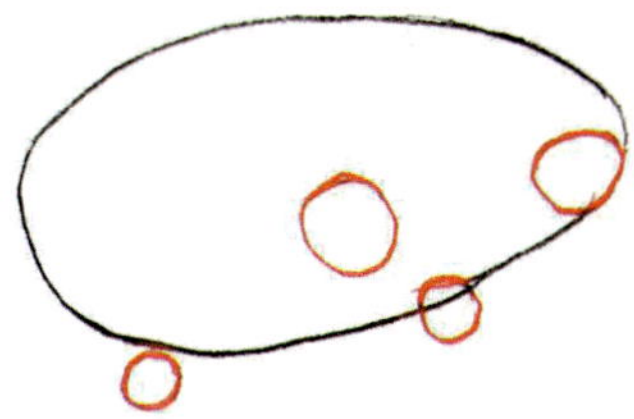

Now, look to the illustration as you draw four small circles. Notice their different sizes and where they are placed inside and outside the oval.

3

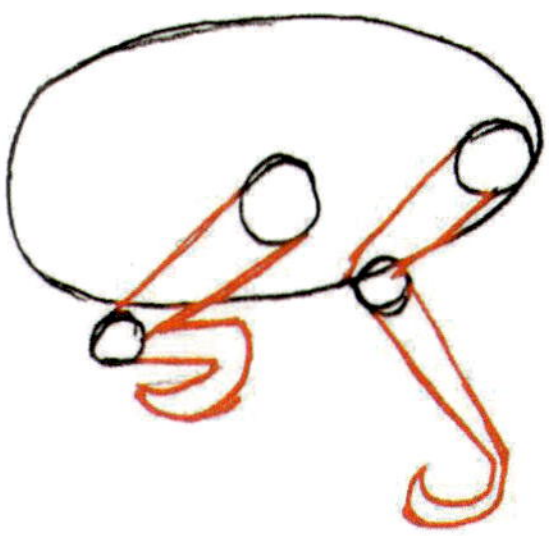

Join the circles with lines to make one front leg and one back leg. The feet should look like hooks as shown.

4

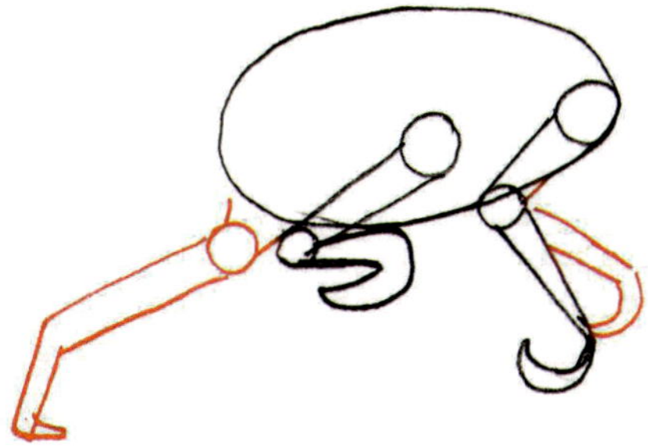

Add a second hook-like leg to the front of the dinosaur. Draw another circle for the second back leg, which will be stretched out. Finish the back leg by drawing in the shapes as shown.

5

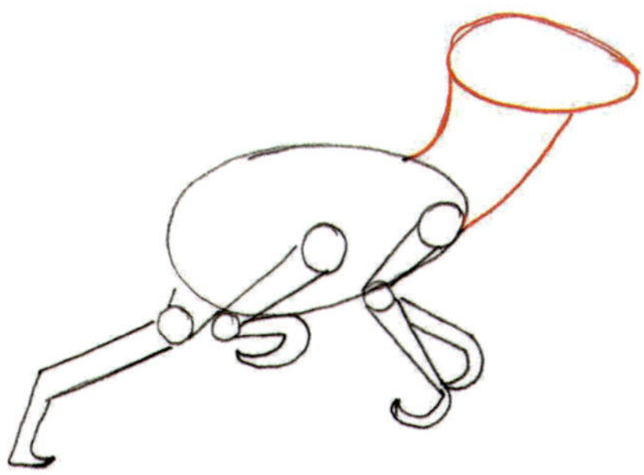

For the head, draw an oval above the body as shown. Make two curved lines from the head to the body for the neck.

6

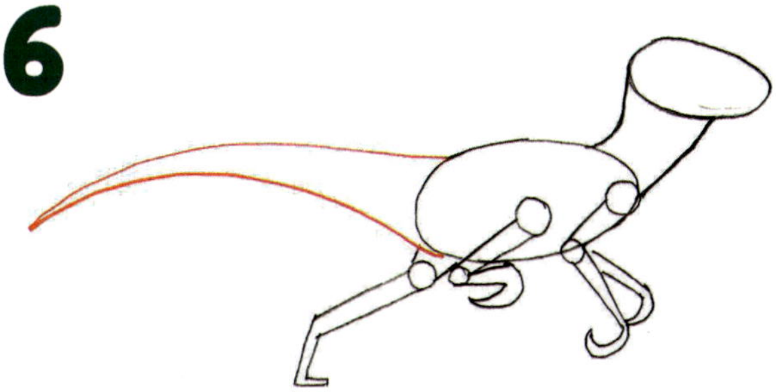

Add the tail by drawing two lines out from the back of the body. These lines should end in a point.

7

Erase any extra lines. Now, draw the eyes, mouth, and nose. For detail, add circles to the body and tail, and shade them in. Your deadly *Deinonychus* is done!

DISCOVER

CAMARASAURUS

Not all dinosaurs were fierce predators. Sauropods were huge, plant-eating dinosaurs with long necks and small heads. Plant-eating creatures are called herbivores. *Camarasaurus* was a sauropod that lived during the Late Jurassic period. *Camarasaurus* weighed up to 20 tons (18.1 mt) and measured about 60 feet (18.3 m) long from head to tail. That sounds big, but compared to other sauropods, like *Brachiosaurus, Camarasaurus* was small!

Camarasaurus had spoon-shaped teeth. Its long neck was perfect for reaching a tasty snack in the tall trees. It ate whole leaves without chewing them. It had holes in its backbones, which made it lighter and put less strain on the huge dinosaur's body.

Camarasaurus may look huge, but it's only a mid-sized sauropod!

1

To begin, draw a large oval to make the body of *Camarasaurus*.

2

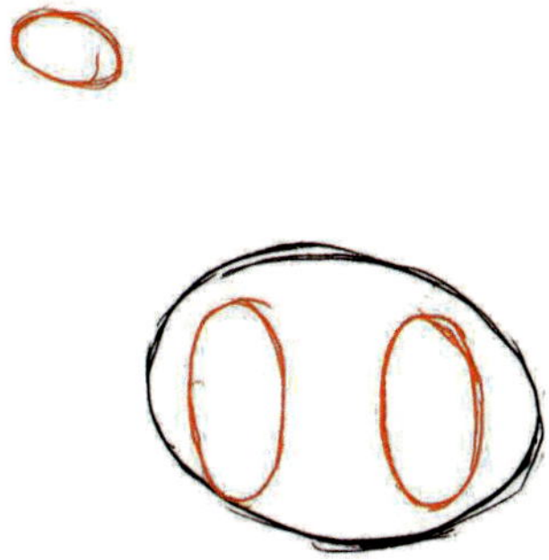

To begin the legs, draw two ovals inside the first oval. Notice where they are placed inside the large oval in the illustration. Then, draw another oval outside the largest oval to the upper left. This smaller oval is the head.

3

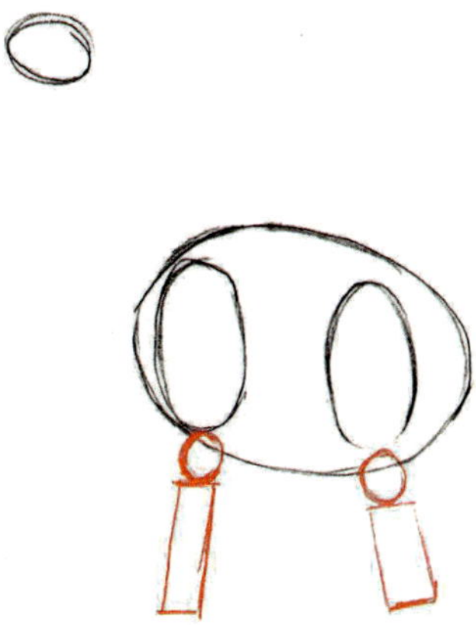

Add two circles and two rectangles below the middle circle for the front legs.

4

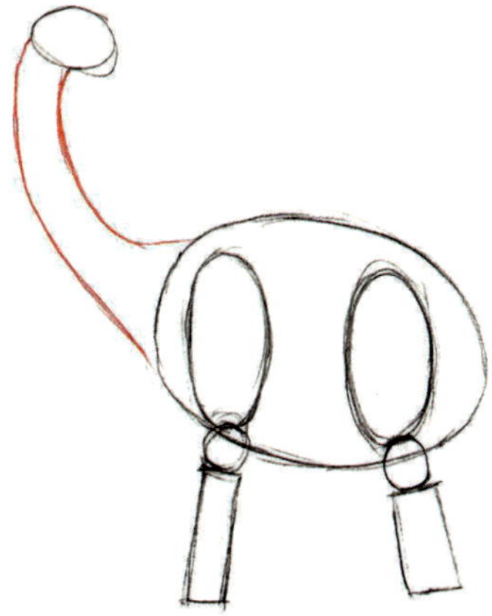

Connect the upper left oval to the body with two curved lines to make the neck.

5

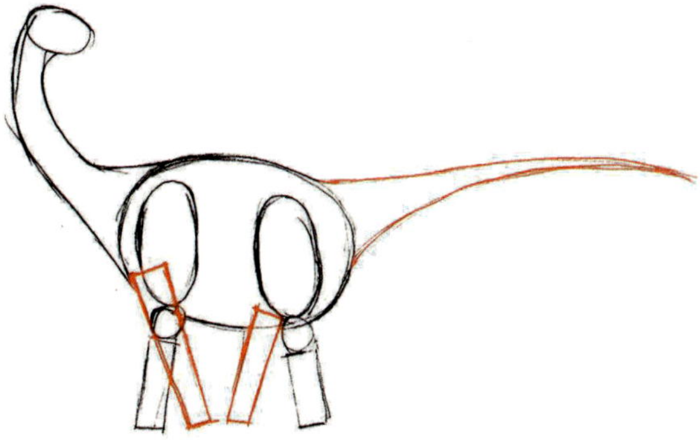

Make two more rectangles coming from the large ovals for the other legs. Draw the tail by making two long, curved lines coming out from the right side of the body. The two lines should come to a point at the end.

6

Clean up the legs by connecting the shapes with curved lines. Finish the face by drawing a line for the mouth and a dot for the eye. Add curved lines to the feet. Erase any extra lines. You've finished your *Camarasaurus*!

DISCOVER BRACHIOSAURUS

Brachiosaurus lived from the Late Jurassic period to the Early Cretaceous period (about 150–130 million years ago). It was a sauropod like *Camarasaurus*, but much bigger!

Brachiosaurus is the heaviest and tallest sauropod for which scientists have found a complete skeleton. It was about 75 feet (22.9 m) long, and at approximately 40 feet (12.2 m) tall, it was one of the tallest of all dinosaurs. It weighed about 89 tons (80.7 mt). This herbivore's long, giraffe-like neck allowed it to reach the tops of trees to eat leaves that many other dinosaurs were unable to reach. It had a small, domed head with a wide, flat nose. Fossils of *Brachiosaurus* have been found in North America, Europe, and Africa.

Brachiosaurus had front legs that were longer than its back legs, like today's giraffes.

1

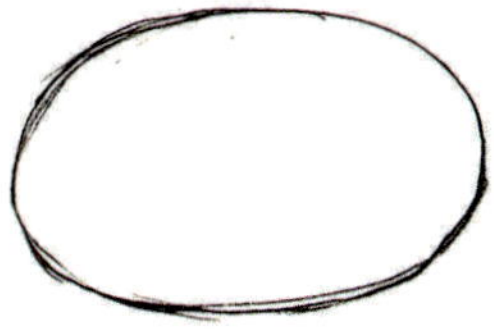

To begin, draw a large oval to make the body of *Brachiosaurus*.

2

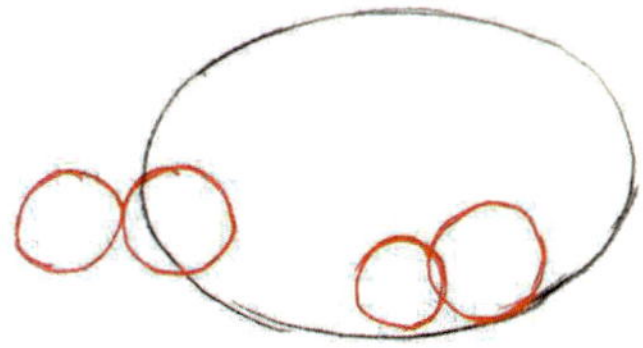

Look to the illustration as you draw four small circles for the legs. Notice where the circles are placed inside and outside the oval.

3

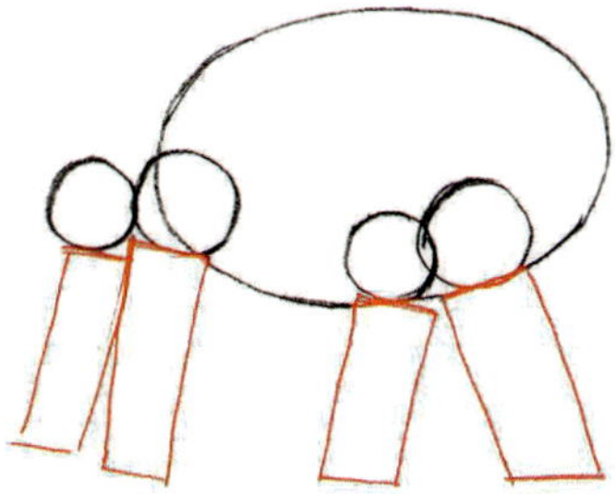

Now, draw four tilted rectangles below the circles to continue the legs.

4

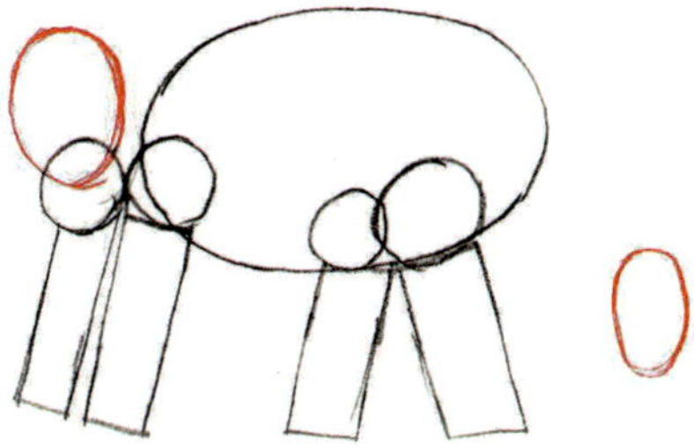

Draw two more small ovals. Place one so it goes through the circle farthest to the left. Draw the other oval to the lower right area of the drawing, away from the rectangles.

5

For the long neck, join these two ovals by drawing two curved lines. Draw the legs by curving the lines of the rectangles.

6

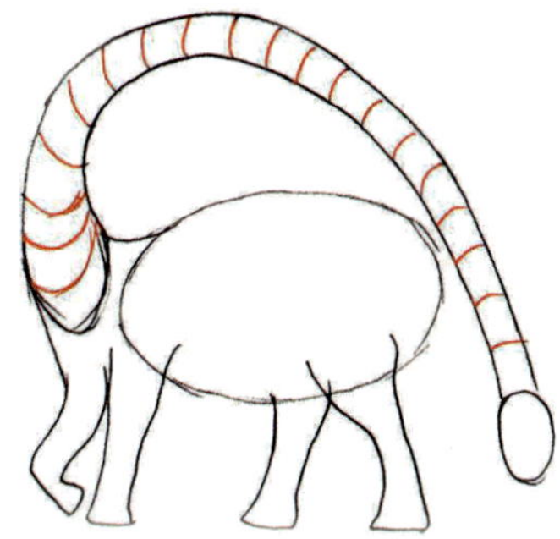

Erase any extra lines, including parts of the circles to clean up the legs. Draw lines inside the neck, as shown in the illustration.

7

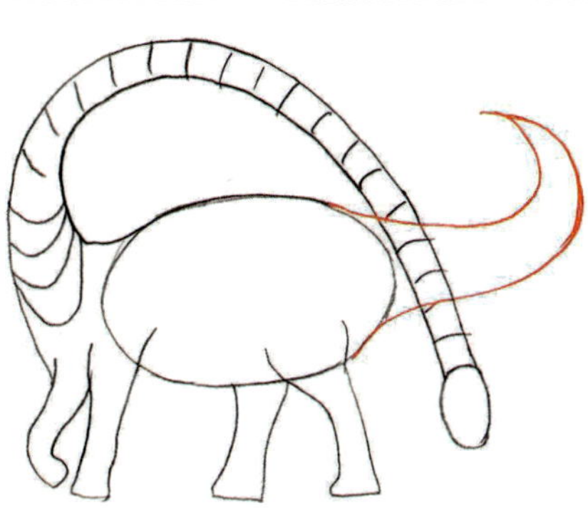

Draw two curved lines out from the back of the body that end in a point to make the tail.

8

Finally, draw an eye, mouth, and nose. Add toes to the feet as shown. Add lines to the front, back, and tail. Draw some plants for it to eat!

DISCOVER STEGOSAURUS

Stegosaurus is a large plant-eating dinosaur best known for the two rows of bony plates that ran down its back. This dinosaur was taller than an African elephant, and could grow up to 30 feet (9.1 m) long. *Stegosaurus* lived during the Late Jurassic period, more than 140 million years ago.

Even though *Stegosaurus* was large, its brain may have been as small as a walnut! Bony plates ran down its neck and back, and it had spikes on its tail. Each of its tail spikes was about 3 feet (0.9 m) long. The spikes may have protected *Stegosaurus* in fights with predators. Scientists aren't sure why *Stegosaurus* had plates, but some say the plates may have helped *Stegosaurus* **regulate** its body temperature.

Early paleontologists believed *Stegosaurus* had plates flat on its back like a turtle! That's why its name means "roofed lizard" in Greek.

1

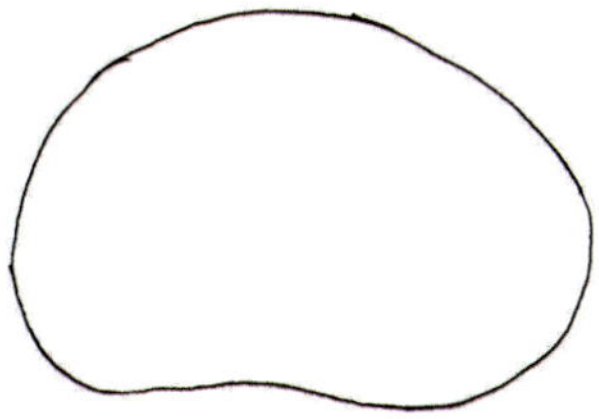

First, draw a large beanlike shape for the body of *Stegosaurus*.

2

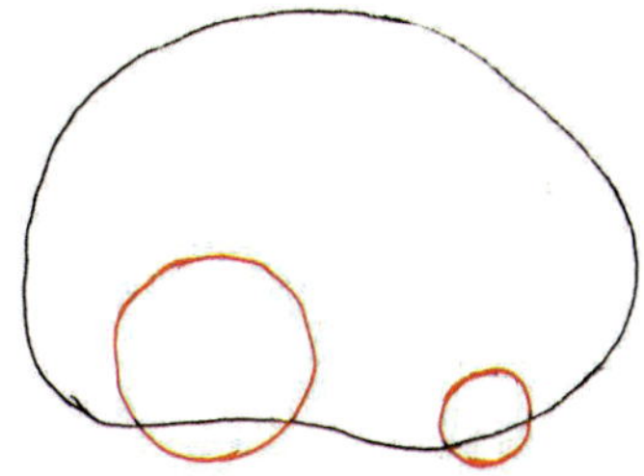

To begin drawing the legs, make two circles at the bottom of the beanlike shape. Notice where they are placed and that one circle is larger than the other.

3

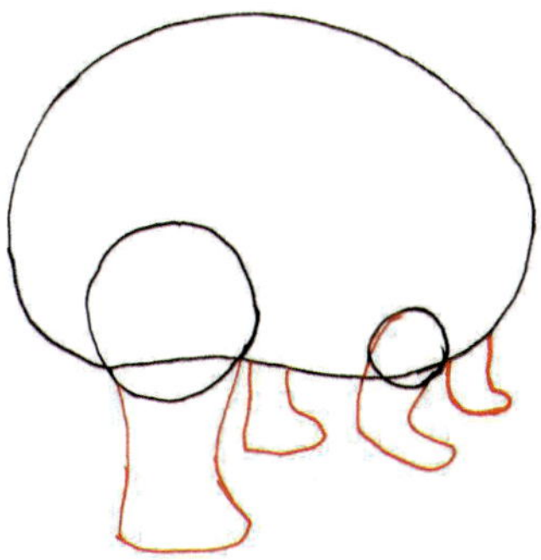

Use the illustration as you draw all four legs as shown. Notice how the front legs are shorter than the back legs.

4

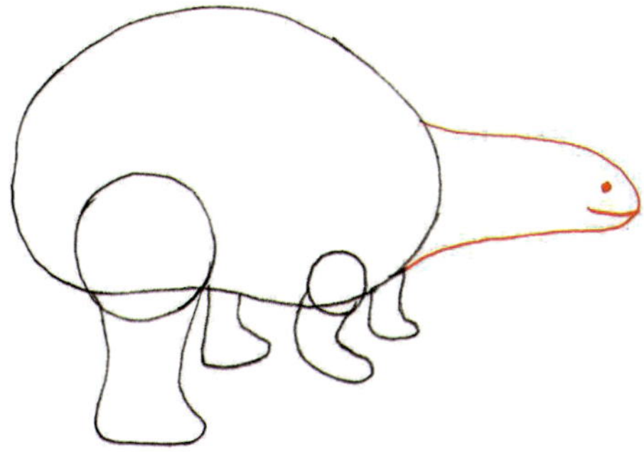

Add a curved shape onto the right side of the body for the neck and head. Add a dot for the eye and a line for the mouth.

5

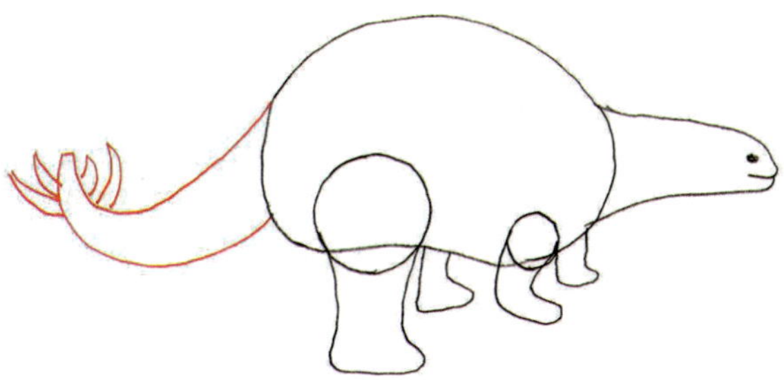

Now, draw the tail by making two long, curved lines from the back, or left, of the body. The two lines should come to a point at the end of the tail. Draw four pointed shapes near the end of the tail for the spikes.

6

Erase the extra lines on the body. To make the plates, draw a set of triangles and a set of diamond shapes on the top, or back, of the body. Notice how the set of triangles runs along the top line of the body. The diamonds join the points of the triangles. That's one special *Stegosaurus*!

DISCOVER STYRACOSAURUS

Just as *Stegosaurus* had spikes on its tail, *Styracosaurus* had spikes on its head. Although *Styracosaurus* was armed with spikes and horns, it did not hunt! Styracosaurus was an herbivore. One long spike, or horn, that was 2 feet (0.6 m) long grew from its nose. *Styracosaurus* had a **frill** on top of its head with between four and six spikes on it.

Styracosaurus lived about 75 million years ago, during the Late Cretaceous period. *Styracosaurus* walked on four legs and weighed up to 3 tons (2.7 mt)! Its **adaptations** helped it survive. For example, its horns and spikes may have helped protect the dinosaur from predators. Its teeth and powerful beak helped it eat tough plants. Many *Styracosaurus* fossils have been found in Alberta, Canada.

Styracosaurus can be identified by the long horn on its nose and its giant spiked frill.

1

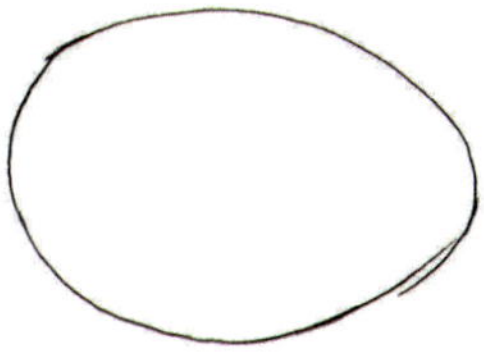

To begin, draw a large oval to make the body of *Styracosaurus*.

2

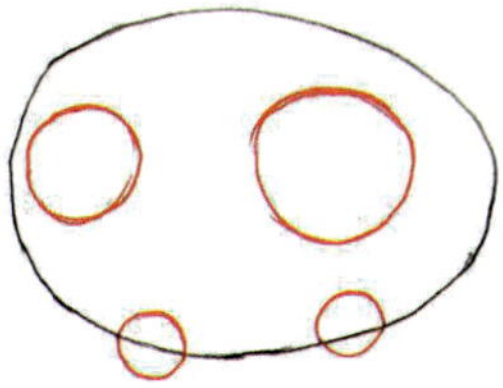

Look to the illustration for guidance as you draw four circles of different sizes inside and overlapping the oval.

3

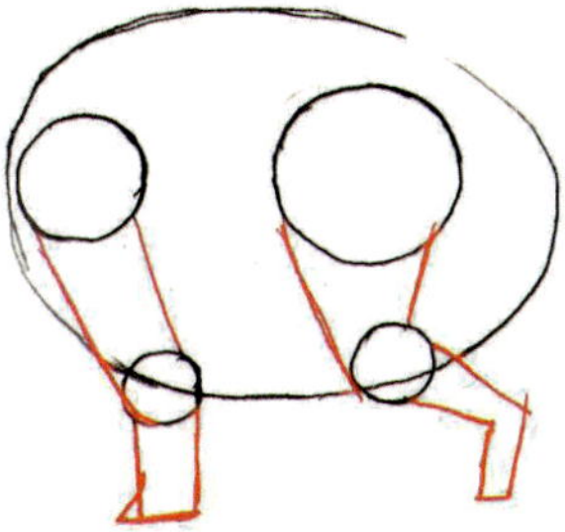

Next, connect the circles with lines to make a front leg, a back leg, and two feet.

4

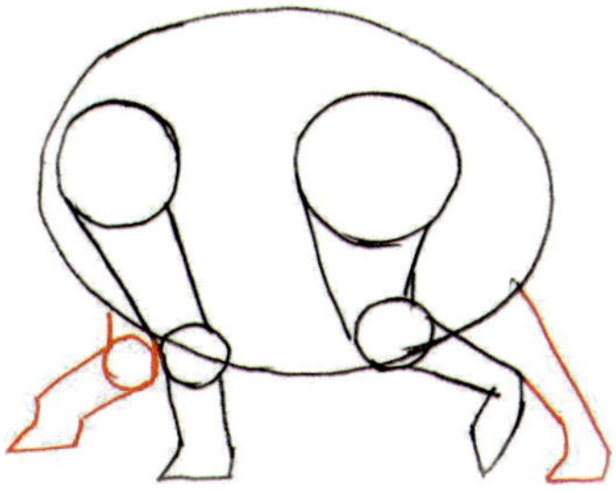

Draw a circle for the other front leg. Then, add lines to finish it. Draw another back leg by making the angular shape as shown.

5

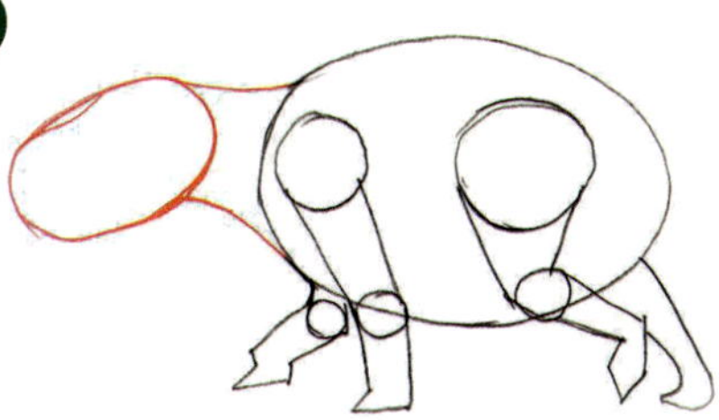

To make the head, draw an oval as shown. Next, draw two curved lines to connect the head to the body.

6

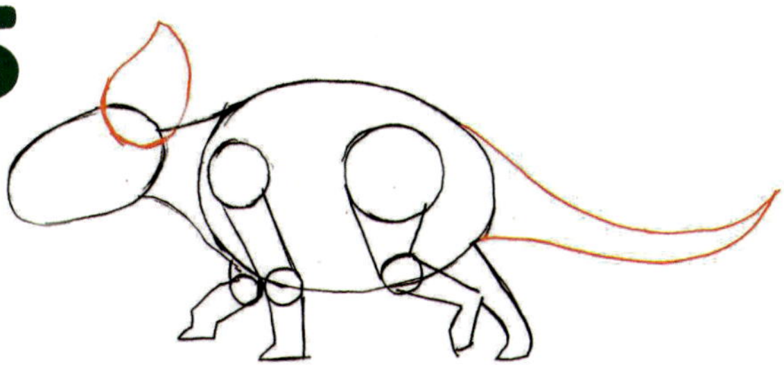

Add a teardrop shape near the top of the head to make the frill. At the right of the oval, add two curved lines that meet at a point for the tail.

7

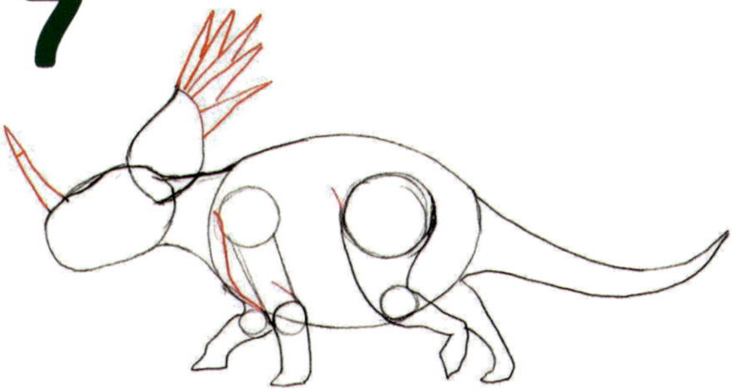

Draw a pointy horn and spikes on the nose and head. Add lines for the legs as shown.

8

Draw the eyes, nose, upper face, and feet. Lastly, erase extra lines. Great job drawing the spiky *Styracosaurus*!

DISCOVER MAIASAURA

Another amazing herbivore was *Maiasaura*. This dinosaur could eat up to 200 pounds (9.1 kg) of plants each day! *Maiasaura* was about 30 feet (9.1 m) long and 8 feet (2.4 m) tall. It weighed about 3 tons (2.7 mt). It had a ducklike bill.

This dinosaur lived during the Late Cretaceous period, about 100 million to 65.5 million years ago. Nests filled with the fossils from adult and young *Maiasaura* have been found in Montana. This find was very exciting for scientists. It proved that *Maiasaura* lived in **colonies** that had large nurseries for their young. The name *Maiasaura* means "good mother lizard." A mother laid 30 to 40 eggs—about the size of ostrich eggs—at once.

Scientists think *Maiasaura* walked slowly on all four legs when looking for food, but ran on its hind legs

1

To begin, draw a large oval to make the body of *Maiasaura*.

2

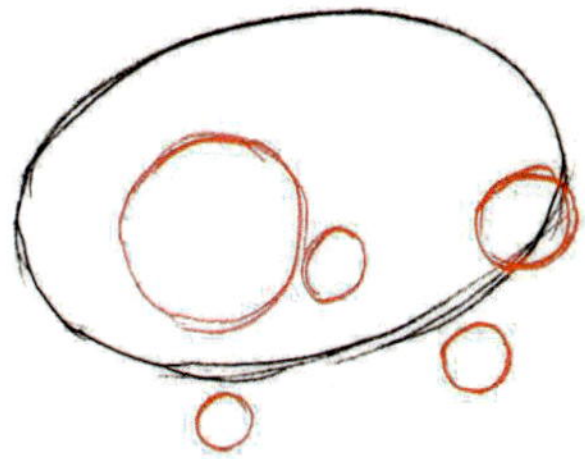

Look to the illustration as you draw five circles. Notice their different sizes and placement.

3

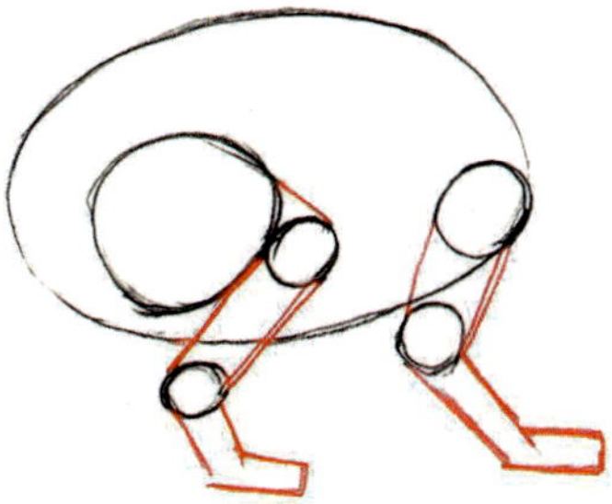

To make one front and back leg, connect the circles with lines as shown.

4

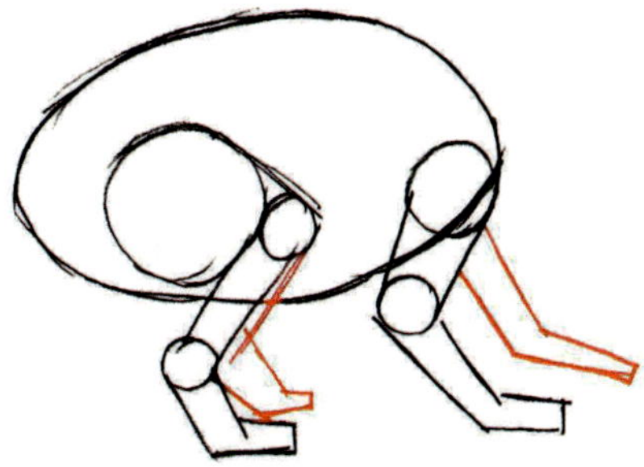

Next, draw the other back and front legs as shown by making similar shapes to the ones you drew in Step 3.

5

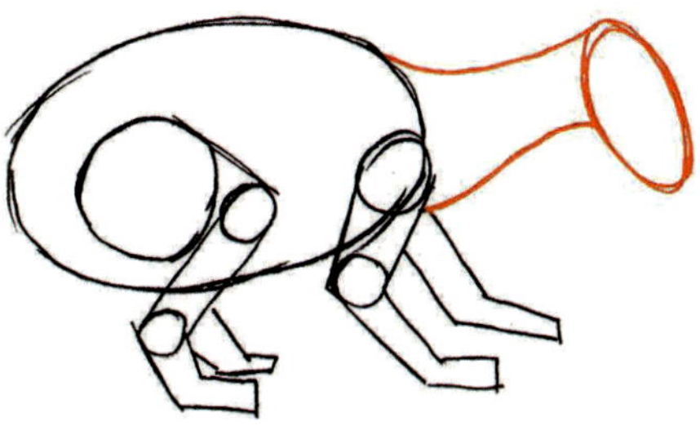

To make the head, draw an oval to the upper-right of the body. Then, add the neck by drawing two curved lines to connect the head to the body.

6

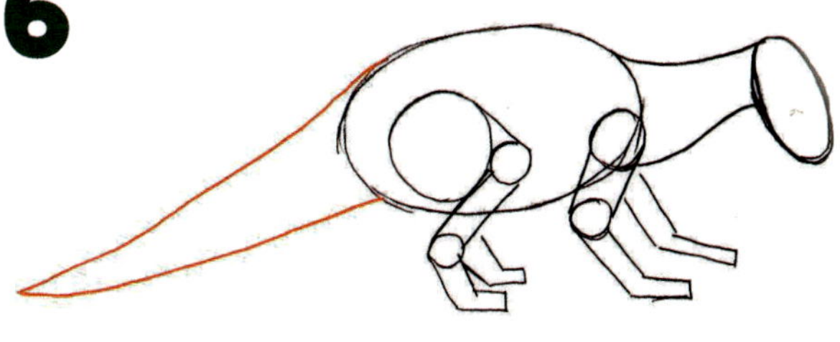

For the tail, draw two lines at the left of the large oval of the body. These lines should come to a point at the end.

7

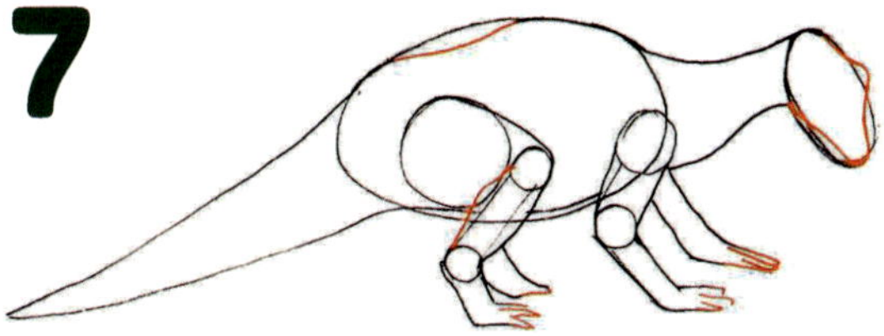

Curve the lines in the legs, body, and head as shown to shape the dinosaur. Draw in the feet. The toes should be pointed.

8

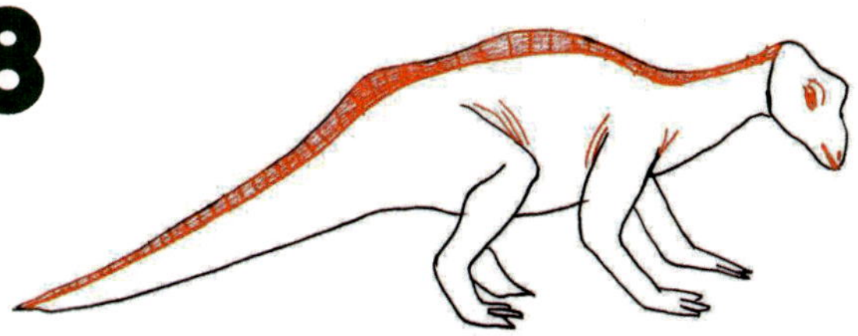

Finally, erase any extra lines. Draw the eyes. After drawing a duckbilled nose, add the mouth. For detail, add a thick stripe along the back, and shade it in. Your mighty *Maiasaura* is done!

GLOSSARY

adaptation: A change in a living thing that helps it live better in its habitat.

colony: A group of living things of the same kind that grow and live together.

evolve: To develop and change over many, many years.

fierce: Given to fighting or killing.

fossil: The hardened remains of a dead animal or plant that lived long ago.

frill: The bony part of an animal that sticks out around its neck like a crown or collar.

mammal: Any warm-blooded animal whose babies drink milk and whose body is covered with hair or fur.

Mesozoic era: A period of history when birds and animals first lived on Earth.

prey: An animal hunted by other animals for food.

raptor: A small to medium-sized predatory dinosaur.

regulate: To fix or adjust the degree or amount of something.

tyrant: A mean ruler.

FOR MORE INFORMATION

WEBSITES

Dinosaur Facts for Kids
www.sciencekids.co.nz/sciencefacts/dinosaurs.html
Explore more amazing facts about dinosaurs and paleontology.

Dinosaurs
kids.nationalgeographic.com/animals/prehistoric
Discover different dinosaurs with National Geographic Kids!

BOOKS

Finn, Peter. *The Ferocious Tyrannosaurus Rex.* New York, NY: Enslow Publishing, 2022.

Kelly, Erin Suzanne. *Dinosaurs.* New York, NY: Children's Press, 2021.

INDEX